Vicinity of Time

Kendall Bradley

Copyright © 2019 by Kendall Bradley

All rights reserved.

ISBN 978-1-62806-262-5 (print | paperback)

Library of Congress Control Number 2019919010

Published by Salt Water Media
29 Broad Street, Suite 104
Berlin, MD 21811
www.saltwatermedia.com

Cover image and author photo courtesy of the author

for RPB
words sometimes fail
the splendor of the tale

and

for Robert
who left us much too soon

*The moon is a house
in which the mind is master
Look very closely:
only impermanence lasts.*

- Sojun

Table of Contents

Having Survived Another Day Of Teaching School, I Wonder What I Am Doing With My Life 1

Ghosts 2

In Oklahoma City On The Day They Dropped A Computer On Mars (1976) 3

Just Us 6

Be Careful 7

After A Long Hard Winter: Daffodils 8

Writer's Block 9

Near an Archaeological Dig Somewhere On The Seaside 10

Jack 11

The Maze 14

Take The Rocks 15

Lucky 16

Eastern Shore 17

Poem To Myself 20

Curves 21

Insight 22

Man In The Moon 23

I-25 24

This Fire	26
Love	27
Pain	28
Heart's Secret Longing	29
Vicinity Of Time	31
Take It As It Comes Or Take It As It Goes	32
Lao Tzu	34
I Looked Up Love	36
What	37
Bukowski	38
First Things First	39
Our Country Now	40
Winter Storm	42
Robert	44
All Too Human	46
La Mer	47
Missing Skip	48
Sometimes	49
The Foxes Of Quinby	50
A Prayer	52
Geometry	53
Metaphysics?	55

Regarding A Recent Headline 56

Why You Just Gotta Love It 57

What Is The Point Of It All? Or, Why Is There Something Rather Than Nothing? 58

When I Go 59

Disembodied Smiles 60

To My Fourth Wife 62

The Right Thing 63

Bad Times 65

To No Avail 66

Beat Down By Life 67

The Mick 69

If Only I Could Find The Words 72

On Thinking About The Impermanence of Things Or Why We Should Make The Most Of Each Day 73

Winter Moonrise 74

Simple Things 75

Whippoorwill 76

Creative Writing Class Assignment: Write A Poem About Sidewalks in 20 Minutes Or Less 77

3 AM 78

January 2017 79

For As Long As You Can 80

Having Survived Another Day Of Teaching School I Wonder What I Am Doing With My Life

It is dusk
and I sit on a stump
of seasoned oak
in front of the barn,
watching the day
fade slowly across
fields heavy with
spring.

In town,
nestled with precision
among stately Victorians
and squat ranchers,
the street lights
begin to flicker
their harmless defiance
at the coming night.

As I light my pipe,
an old sedan
explodes by,
the ugly staccato
of its torn muffler
rips through my veins
with the senseless
violence of sudden
acceleration.

When it is gone,
finally swallowed by a long
stretch of crushed stone,
the wind still ripples
the tall, slim-stemmed oats
in front of me, bending
incomprehensible
patterns toward
the darkened woods.

Ghosts

They gather
in moonlight
like wisps of memory
congregating
where back roads
stub out on the verge
of bayside guts.

They orgy
in their own
flickering way
among discarded
beer cans and used
condoms, fast food
wrappers and the gutted
carcasses of deer.

Their voices
are made of wind
and they take succor
however they may
as they move
into salt marsh
or pine woods

seeking untold things
in the crevices of night,
hurrying
to consummate
their secret deeds

before dawn's first
sunlight shimmer
of bejeweled
spartina.

In Oklahoma City On The Day They Dropped A Computer On Mars (July 20, 1976)

I
Wind
whistles through
skull eyes
and fire
covers
the plains.

The armies
move slowly,
relentlessly,
maybe ten miles a year
over rock
and brush sage.

Ranchers fear
them, fear they
will cross
the river
and want them
destroyed,
debating poison
or napalm.

II
Beneath
city streets
and camper parks,
beneath
McAlester, Guthrie,
Chickasha, all
the little towns
invisibly burning
out of control,

the prairie sleeps.
Its breathing
is quiet, steady,
difficult to hear.
Even an old
hunter of buffaloes,
lying ear to the earth
would not discern
the subtle rhythm
of its ancient life,
its restless wanderings
in dream.

III
What does
the prairie dream?
Gnarled old elms
and riverbank
cottonwoods do not say.
The wind at dusk
gives no clues.

Water,
prairie water
pumped from
Oklahoma City reservoir
is warm
at the tap,
thick with chlorine.
Life departed from its molecules
many yearsago.
It has no secrets
to tell,
no subterranean
messages to give.
It has lost contact
with the prairie's
dreams.

It is dead
water.

IV
The ants
blanket twenty
square miles
of Texas prairie.

They feel
the quiet breathing,
they know and share
the secret dreams.
As they journey
to the river,
the fire armies listen
to their mother's
voice.

Just Us

Let time
be a place
in which
we hold
each other
for awhile

no past
no future
no pretensions

just us
for now.

Be Careful

- to my sons

Don't let
the tiny mouths
get you,
the ones that
cheer like
clouds
and smile
like polished
stars.
Don't get cut
by the broken
pieces of
light
forming cities
of no return,
with dark streets
turning back
upon themselves,
upon you.
Don't get lost
in the soft
under belly
of a lie,
thinking you
finally are
safe.

After A Long Hard Winter: Daffodils

These early
bright yellow
flowers
spring from
the still cold
dark earth,
random as
sorrows,
yet sweet
beyond measure
in their brief
rage of
beauty.

Writer's Block

For better or worse,
I have things I want
to say.

But the proverbial
blank page
stares back at me
more empty than
a nihilist's universe.

I try to coax
out the words
with promises
of clarity, power,
even exultation.

Promises, promises.

The words are
too smart
for that, or
too ornery.

They have
their own agenda.
They're probably lounging
on a white sand beach
somewhere far away,
knocking back gin
and tonics
and lasciviously
watching the Girl from Ipanema.

No doubt,
they're holding out
for inspiration –

it certainly can't be
for money or fame.

Near An Archaeological Dig Somewhere On The Seaside

My spirit moves
through interstices,
peers into dark,
hollow places,
lifts the smooth
edges of dreams.

It soars through
cloud layers
of prehistoric bone
to dance
in solar wind.

Back to earth
it flies,
to forest and stream,
to dirt and stone.

It becomes an owl
perched on a black
limb in the dusk
and with owl eyes
watches as the night
moves in over
the marsh.

Jack

1.
Jack of some trades
master of none
Jack is
nimble
Jack is quick
but Jack refuses
to play the game.

Wanting no label
seeking no fame
who to praise
and who to blame?

2.
All politicians lie
because they must,
at the very least
because they must.

But the world
moves along
over the streams and rivers,
over the mountains
and stark cliffs
over the parched
deserts
of the centuries,

through the teeming cities,
through gardens
and used car lots,
over the oceans,
through the cyberspace
of the years,

the world moves along
over the corpses
of dead politicians.

3.
Journey charted
or uncharted,
nameless teleology
or dead end,
who can tell?
The noisy world,
the cacophony,
the voices that never stop
in the city streets
in the wilderness

the voices of charlatans
and pundits,
of prophets and priests,
the inhuman voice
of history itself.

Turn down the volume
mute the buzz
and look for
the jester's dance
like in days of old
in the courts of kings.

The jester's frozen,
knowing, mocking grin
tells us all
we need to know.

4.

Sacred and profane,
holy and unholy...
a false dichotomy.
There is no such thing
as salvation,
because the rules
have changed.

Jack can be nimble
and Jack can be quick
but Jack knows too well

there is no
candlestick.

The Maze

Not life's
twistings and turnings,
but we ourselves
are the maze

and the lurking
Minotaur
we have placed there,
awaiting our missteps
with savage horns,

is as real
as any illusion
can be.

Take The Rocks

Take the rocks,
any rocks,
jagged or smooth
as long as they are
unrelentingly hard
and along the sea coast.

And let the sea be just itself,
no more no less,
neither mournful
nor savage nor strange.

And the sea birds
will be there
curlews, terns, and gulls
buffeting the wind
and crying their cries.

Look hard and you
will always find
a few of us there
with more on the way,

inexplicably
waiting in line
to beat ourselves
against the rocks
as the sea birds cry
their natural cries,

beating and beating
until the bruises come
until the bones break
until the brain matter
and the fecal matter
spew forth
into the sea.

Lucky

Most of the time
we don't even know
the right questions,
much less
the right answers.

But sometimes
we simply
somehow
luck out.

For instance,
you are both
the right question
and the right answer
for me.

Just call me Lucky.

Eastern Shore

Pleistocene glacier spawn,
sea ooze, unconsolidated
silt and sand,
wind cast and storm swept
along the narrow
10,000 year old spine
stretched taught
between bay and sea,
dark streams flowing
east or west,
freshwater to salt,
winding creeks to tidal flats,
high marsh and low marsh
and oyster grounds,
barrier islands
on the Atlantic side
holding back the wild sea
yet moving, ever shifting
to the sea's command,
and on the bayside,
the wide creeks
leading to the deep
blue of the Chesapeake…

On the mainland
old growth forests of oak,
beech, black gum
and sycamore
now nearly gone,
loblolly pine
still sending tap roots deep,
seeking a way to thrive
near encroaching
salt marsh
and rising tides.

Gentle swale and undulation,
whale wallows,
broad fields of loamy sand
and sandy loam,
soils called Nimmo
and Polawana, Munden,
Bojac, and Molena,
potato and tomato land,
soy and barley
and spring wheat,
field corn which
dances beneath
autumn moons,
the bayside strawberry fields
long gone, the cropping
of yams and Haymans,
peas, onions, and squash,
mostly now
gray haired memories,

potstone and plough shards,
Algonquian flint
and musketballs,
mule skulls and bear jaws,
rusted shackles—
the earthy secrets
of the centuries
sometimes revealed,
blood and oaths
sometimes recalled,
the ghostly demarcations,
the King's patents,
the metes and bounds,
the stolen land
aggrandized,
bought and sold
but never possessed
by transits and rods

by macadam and asphalt
by tar and chip and concrete
by rail beds and power grids
by cul de sacs and billboards
by Walmart and Food Lion
by poultry houses
by combines and tractors
by crop dusters and four wheelers
by neon lights and traffic lights
by street lights and headlights...

for the land abides.

Ever waiting
between sea and bay,
the land abides,
ever dreaming
its *terra firma* dreams
the land abides,
beneath the stars
beneath the sun
beneath the moon

the land abides
while still it may.

Poem To Myself

The two AM moon rises,
a fiery wreck
from some forgotten sea,
as loblolly
and sweet gum
tear songs
from this westerly gale.
I stand barefoot
on the cold
kitchen floor,
fleeing dreams
to drink a glass
of cool water
from a deep well.

What a night
to walk in the woods
raising old bones
from their forgetful sleep!
What a night to lie there
unheard and unseen,
an imperceptible shadow
motionless
among darker shadows
dancing...

Curves

Curve of space
curve of time,

infinity of sky
particularity of earth.

Your skin
holds many
secrets.

Curve of breast
curve of thigh,

my tongue traces
the outline
of you,

knowing more
than it can say.

Insight

It is as if
a lightning strike
has turned the whole
world
into a photographic
negative,
capturing a single
moment of
incandescent truth
turned inside out.

Inside the negative,
we are shadows
dancing
in the cool
aftermath of light.

We dream
of air,
we reach
with darkened limbs
for something
undefined,
untouched,
something beyond
the borders.

Man In The Moon

The day has faded
and the moon
has floated in
and sits in a chair
in the nearly empty
darkening room
on the second floor.

The moon looks out
the tall open window
at the vacated sky
and smiles
as only the moon
can smile.

Outside, a wispy girl
with periwinkle eyes
walks along
the narrow street

singing to the moon
like the sea
will sometimes
sing,
an enticing song
of wind and wave.

The moon
lights a cigar
and ignores the girl
thinking only

of tequila
and curvy women
in smoky bars

and why the world
seems to need
so very, very much.

I-25

The lonely and spooky
late night interstate
from Los Cruces
to Albuquerque

is good
for talk radio
or rock oldies
or just thinking
thoughts random
as tumbleweeds
as the desert miles
slip by.

Truckers run it in
three hours or less
but it takes me
nearly four.

Out along the looming
mesas and winding
canyons,
I pass the lights
of Radium Springs
and Hatch,
Truth or Consequences,
and Elephant Butte.

In the dark stretch
between Rock Canyon
and Socorro
I expect to see
phantom hitchers,
the Walking Dude,

or dark-eyed aliens
with big heads
and little arms
coming down
steep arroyos.

Instead,
a few shards
of busted big rig tires
and the occasional
shell-crushed body
of an unlucky
armadillo
splayed on
the shoulder

is all I see

before finally
crossing
the Rio Grande
and passing north
along the bright
incandescence of
the South Valley.

This Fire

This fire
that burns me
is elemental, primeval,
older than
the earth.

It is white
hot,
yet still a smolder,
waiting for the quick
burst of
flame.

And when
the flames come,
I wonder if
this will be
a controlled burn

or conflagration,

a super nova
lighting up
star systems
throughout
the galaxy
of our lives?

Love

Some try
for a lifetime
and come up
short
not knowing why.

Others try
to get it all
at once
like a hit
of smack
and keep
coming back
for the rush
that rushes on.

Some get there
too soon
and don't
even know
they made it
until it's
just too, too
late.

Some swear
they don't
need it,
don't want it.

Who are *they*
trying to kid?

Pain

What is pain?
Just a message
to the brain.

No pain,
no gain
is what
they say.

But Pain says
give me a name,
any name,

and I can make
that person cry

enough!

Broken bones,
broken hearts,
broken dreams...

Try to gain
all you want,
I can break you,

says Pain,

and just
so you know

I can be
very creative
very resourceful

and I'll find you,
trust me,
in any of the places
you may ever
dare to hide.

Heart's Secret Longing

Sometimes,
in the quiet
of our most hidden
and repressed lives,
when the noises
we live by suddenly
fade out,
leaving us
with the blunt fact
of ourselves,
the heart's
secret longing
can become a
clandestine voice

speaking to us

like a soft
but restless wind
in pines at dusk,
like the sound
of distant surf
on barrier islands
out of the mainland's
reach,

like a faint crying
in the marsh
at the edge
of our dreams.

The furtive heart...
such a dangerous thing.

How do we gauge
its truth or deceit?

When told
our heart's
secret longing,
how do we know
if we should
pay attention

or pretend
we just don't
hear?

Vicinity Of Time

The universe
as the mind of God...

the universe
as a membrane,
one among many
folded into
layers of infinite
possibility...

the universe
as too big
or perhaps too small
to ever comprehend.

You and I
in our own
vicinity of time,
in our own hard won
outpost of space

here in this room

drinking wine,
touching each other
with our hands,
with our lips

letting the universe
be a sparrow's eye,
an equation,
a madman's dream,

whatever it must.

Take It As It Comes Or Take It As It Goes

Here comes the world!
Here comes life,
oozing its way from
murky depths
to embattled shores

and so forth and so on
and eons later
here WE come,
homo sapiens
evidence of progress
pinnacle of the process,
the two legged packets
of walking, talking quanta,
temporary vessels of empty space
held together by the music
of vibrating strings
so small they can be detected
only by a theory

and we are loud
very loud for temporary
vessels of empty space
very loud for mere theories

as we clog the corridors
of the ages with
our great importance,
an endless stream of
loud whirling dervishes
roaring like the wind
making IT all up as we go

trying to make IT
go a little bit further
a little bit longer
a little bit better
or just trying to make IT at all

not even knowing
why we are here
and why we are doing
ALL THIS STUFF
and making all this noise.

Look out!
Here we come
in all our glory,
we the wind roarers,
we the vessels
of empty space,
we the vibrating strings
with mouths.

Lao Tzu

The Tao that can be told is not the eternal Tao
– from The Tao Te Ching

I
Even though scholars
say you may never
have existed,
this is how
I like to think of you:

It is early spring.
The cedars are still
heavy with snow,
but the dark stream
is running strong
and free.
You cross the icy
torrent with silent
ease and move up
the far bank
on a winding path,
a careful, watchful
man, young for
your years.

If this were a landscape
painting, you would be
the tiny, solitary figure
nearly lost in the vastness
of mountains and snow.

But, you are not lost
and, soon,
somewhere between

heaven and earth,

and a thousand peaks
from palace intrigues
and temples of jade,
you will be
drinking warm tea
in a dry hut.

II
Or let's say
you never existed.
The words were
written by others.
The paradoxical words
which belie themselves,
the words which say
the eternal Tao
cannot be described
by words.
No blame for you.

III
No, I like to think
you did exist.
As for the words,
you knew the geese
would fly,
the snow would
fall,
and water would seek
its own level
without the words.
The hearts of men,
adrift in the sea
of ten thousand
things, needed
the words
that you would
never write.

I Looked Up Love

- for Ronda

I looked up *love*
in the dictionary
of my heart
and found old
words with smooth
round sounds,
ancient syllables
reminding me
of your eyes
when I awake
to find you
gazing at me.

I looked up *love*
in the dictionary
of my mind
and entered
a room without walls
or floor or ceiling
only a doorway
into diffused light
and infinite air
and you reading
poetry to me
without speaking
words.

I looked up *love*
in the dictionary
of my soul
and found an ancient
fire forcing back
the darkness
of myself,
displaying symbols
words cannot reach,
allowing me
to see your face
in the dancing
of the Light.

What

Is it the intent
or the outcome?
The tree
or the shadow
of the tree?
Is it the sun
that burns
the wheat
or the sun
that warms
the ground
and makes
the wheat
grow?

Is it the smell
of your hair
and the taste
of you?
Or the memory
of it all
at four AM
with thunder
and lightning
on the bay
and the street light
coming in
my window
for all the world
like moonlight?

Bukowski

His sorry mug was
the face of the damned
and he wielded words
like a weapon of despair.
I disdained him at first,
thinking his poems
too uncouth, depraved
and raw.
Yet the more I read
the more the demented
truth sank in:
his words were holy
like a light bulb is holy,
like a backyard
clothesline is holy,
like the inside of
a beer can is holy
and filled with a
universe of debauched
butterflies.

He was an
alley cat of words,
Old Tom hard on
the scent of all the pussy
on the block,
roses springing from
his urine sprays,
diamonds turning up
years after his death
on the rainy and
psychotic neon streets
of forever.

First Things First

First:
we must love
ourselves,
unconditionally.

This is not
egotistical
and it is not
easy.

True self love
is acceptance
of imperfection

in all of its many
guises.

Then:
we are free
to love others,
also unconditionally.

In this way,
our own shadows
do not diminish
the light
of love.

Our Country Now

It is not that
the center will not hold,
it is that there is no center,
no still point
as our world spins
out of control,
no middle ground of
possible compromise

another civil war,
not geographical
but ideological,

a fissure of the national spirit
and it could be even
worse than the last time.

No bodily carnage,
no bloody ground,
no Gettysburg or Antietam,
yet a fight for the very
soul of the country
seems to be underway.

How else do we explain
propagandists running wild
through the streets
of cyberspace,
reason vanquished
as if traitorous,
hope turned to scorn,
love hated
and hatred loved,
decency decried,

leaders vilified
and villains leading,

the minds of innocents
laid waste with weapons
of mass destruction,
not bombs or viruses,
but myths clutched so tightly
they have become
twisted and deformed

ready to burst
ready to explode
ready to trench out
an unbridgeable chasm,
an abyss so black
and bottomless

it could be,
but *must* it be

the future of America?

Winter Storm

It is cold dark
and the old bones
of this house
moan in pain
as this winter nor'easter
has its fierce way,
showing no mercy
even to the ghosts
who will not
venture abroad tonight
but rather
have taken up their
tenuous habitation
inside my own skull
to ramble and sulk,
accuse, decry and defame
as they see fit.

The storm storms on
with ice, sleet, and snow
as we lie together,
warm in a heatless room,
twelve years to the night
we slept together
for the first time
choosing a new life,
becoming quiet,
tainted heroes
to ourselves and
anathema to those we hurt.

As the roiling sea
cuts new inlets
through the barrier islands,
destroys fishing piers
in tourist towns,

and sends saltwater
darkly into the streets
of Wachapreague and
Chincoteague,

I think back those twelve years
to the sharp joy and
exquisite pain
of those days,
to our own storm of storms,
knowing that
if need be I would
do it all again,
take the wild risk
again and again
over and over forever,

and now wondering

had we not chosen
as we did,
had not chosen
the sweet hope of our love
over any consequence,

where would
I be now
and how well
would I be coping
with even the basic
simple things

such as a night-long
raging wind
or the inevitable
sun-bright calm
to follow?

Robert

The tears do not come as
often anymore,
but time is no healer,
it is at best
a kind of desultory
anesthesiologist.

We didn't know
that for you it was not
a question of *if*
but of *how* and *when*
and you fooled us all.

You left us,
the loved ones,
aka the ones that loved,
trapped on the other side
of our own mercy,
angry and chastising
yet mournful, forlorn,
and racked with all
the standard
self-recriminations
and what ifs,

consumed by
the vexing, sucking desire
to make sense
of the inexplicable,
the relentless need to force
the issue blindly onward
even if to no avail
and finally,
in spite of our own
best intentions,

not really giving up,
but ending up
in exhausted frustration
with no compelling
exegesis

only the bare, blunt,
immutable
and irreducible fact
of what you planned

and what you did.

All Too Human

I don't believe
the average American
needs an assault rifle
and I detest the ugly
power of the NRA,
but tonight,
after six break-ins
in two weeks
in our little town of 408 citizens,
I load my three shot
12 gauge Mossberg pump
and my five round
32 revolver for the first time,
put them carefully
in the closet
near the bed,
and head downstairs
to dinner,
the sweet but
unfamiliar smell
of gun oil
still strong
on my hands.

La Mer

I would write
a eulogistic poem
about you
as so many
have done

but when I walk
beside you
on the moon strand
in the wind mist

I am overwhelmed
not by the romance
of your dark presence,
but by your vast otherness
and by what I fear
may be
your total lack
of intrinsic meaning.

Mother of all living
organisms on planet earth,
progenitor of
metaphor and myth,
how can this be?

In your presence,
I am muted
into uneasy silence.

I feel that I am
but a vagrant
on the dangerous shores
of your mercy,
making,
in spite of myself,
wordless supplication
to your
uncanniness

and to mine.

Missing Skip

When you came to us,
driven by instinct
and desperation,
you were no bigger
than a quick whisper.
You chose us
against our will
but we could not
let you starve
and we tried our best
to do right by you.

In return,
you brought us
unexpected magic.

Little did we know
that the exchange
of gifts
would be so lopsided
in our favor.

And little did we know
after only three months
and ten days with us,
after you left
for your new home
four hours away
on a farmette
in Mongomery County, MD,
that the deck, the porch,
the yard, and every
room in our house
would be so
devastatingly emptied

of your bright presence,
our hearts so
immeasurably full

of such implacable
sadness.

Sometimes

Beyond the darkness,
death's light

a force field
of fire.

I move like a moth,
in spiraling
circles

ever closer
to the flame,

yearning
for the final
burn out

once and for all

neither to be
nor not to be.

The Foxes of Quinby

The old heads
have never seen
anything like it.

They have been
showing up inexplicably
on front porches,
along the main street,
and under the culverts
at Bradford Acres.

Somebody said
coyotes have moved in
to Cat's Point
driving them out
of the woods.

No one knows for sure
but there are kittens
and toddlers to protect
and great grandmothers
who must walk to their sheds
for sundry things.

So the men take
target practice and
the trophy kills mount up,

but the foxes keep
coming,
out of the woods
out of the fields
into the yards
and driveways
in broad daylight.

They arrive
with an unexpected
nonchalance
and they are chased away
with shovels or shot

dead with a certain
exuberance.

Animal Control is no help
and the Game Commission
doesn't care
and the Health Department
is only interested in rabies.
Bring in the dead foxes
and we will saw
off their heads, they say,
and send them
for testing
to the Norfolk lab.

But rabies is not
really suspected,
as the foxes are not foaming
at the mouth or attacking
indiscriminately.
They are just showing up
at odd times and places
for no apparent reason.

So the trophy kills
mount up
as the foxes keep coming
with a kind
of relentless abandon
and their eyes
are as dark
as the night woods,
as dark as the marsh
with daylight faded,

as dark
as the wild blood
that drips down
the reddish fur
onto the ground
beside whitewashed
sheds in the Quinby
moonlight.

A Prayer

Please save me
from the
disingenuous
smiles
of those who
always know
a better way.

Please save me
from the cute ones
who laugh loudest
at their own jokes.

Please save me
from those
who would
do me harm
by doing me
good.

Please save me
from those
who would have
me saved.

But most of all,
please save me from
myself
as I pitch, weave,
and stumble

through
the jumbled,
uncertain landscape
of my own good
intentions.

Geometry

- with apologies to Euclid

The circle knows
the still point
of the turning world
and rectangles
tend to have OCD.

You may rarely see
squares and irregular
polygons
hanging out

but it seems
that both groups
are into their own
special brand
of kink.

Better not trust
triangles
and their sharp
teeth, say
the trapezoids.

Octagons
and hexagons
discuss philosophy

while pentagons,
we all know,
make war.

Who knows
what the tetrahedrons think
in their secret lives?

Dodecahedrons
like Greek food
and parakeets

but the parabolas want
to know:
who will save us
from the straight lines?

Metaphysics?

The present,
specious or not,
always here
and yet never here,
disappears before
I can even write
these words.

It instantly
becomes the past,
a collection of
ghostly forms
without habitation
in time or space,
accessed only by
the constant
interpretation
of bias.

The future,
by definition,
never happens
and never will.

Son of a bitch!

Regarding A Recent Headline

Nor'easter,
sudden squall,
dead calm

the sea can kill.

Old salts know
the deep longing
of the sea

and its
ultimate indifference

once it's had
its way.

Last week,
another body
washed up
on the bayside
shore

and they are looking
for one more

and the sleek
craft, or pieces
thereof,

not so seaworthy
after all.

Why You Just Gotta Love It

Love is not always
what it is cracked
up to be.

It can be a jackal,
a piranha, a serial
killer,

a cunning imposter.

Give it half a chance
and it will rip
your veins out,
make your toes bleed,
or run you up
a flag pole naked
for the whole
world to see.

Love will turn
you inside out
and hang you from
a tree limb,
tickle your exposed
organs with moonbeams
and then cut you up
into little pieces
for the crows.

Try to tell
the story of love
and it will stampede
your similes,
scalp
your metaphors,
make you sound
like a wheezing moron
on a dead run
for your life.

What Is The Point Of It All? Or, Why Is There Something Rather Than Nothing?

The metaphysicians
are good at raising
the questions
but terrible at
providing
the answers.
Has Plato
or Aristotle
or Kant
or Heidegger really
told us the point
of it all?

Don't get me wrong,
neither has Darwin
or Einstein
or Bertrand Russell

or Homer or Joyce
or Dostoyevsky,

or Jesus or Mohammed
or The Buddha
and all the rest.

While the sun still shines
and the earth still
moves on its axis,
the trees
still do their things
and the birds
still do theirs

and we still do ours...

and most of the time
most of us
just don't think
about it.

It's probably for the best.

When I Go

Let it be
cremation for me

no box
under the ground

no slow
decomposition

and feast of worms.

Let the
hungry flames

have their way
with me.

I only wish
it could be

a back yard
bonfire

beneath all
the stars

of a clear
winter sky.

Disembodied Smiles

Once while walking
down the street,
I happened to look up
to see
disembodied smiles
floating in the air
like so many
party balloons,

moving slowly
out of reach,
heading for
the jetstream,

all the smiles
of the world
or so it seemed:

smug smiles
fake smiles
happy smiles
forced smiles
quizzical smiles
perplexed smiles
wicked smiles
paradoxical smiles
naughty smiles
facetious smiles
bold smiles
self-effacing smiles
tentative smiles
beneficent smiles
reluctant smiles
sinister smiles

smiles of rapture
smiles of pain
smiles for all occasions

all the smiles
of the world
moving up, up,

and away.

To My Fourth Wife

Red wine
and sweet jazz,
Delta blues
and seedy bars,
Key West
and the front porch.
We shoot pool,
discuss philosophers,
kings and JFK.

When we make love,
the gods are jealous.

You slay me
with your eyes
and revive me
with a kiss.
You make me
coq au vin
while I write
you poems
which never say
quite enough,
no matter
how hard I try.

The Right Thing

The world
isn't so screwed up
because so many
of us
just don't do
the right thing.

It's screwed up
because so many
of us are
actually doing
what we
consider to be

the right thing.

The problem is
that most of the time
we really just don't know
what the right thing is.

The right thing
is hard to pin down.
We can tell that
just by observing
how screwed up
it all gets

when people
with different ideas
of the right thing
try to kill
each other.

It just seems
the more certain
we are about
the right thing
and the more
we force it on others,

the less right it becomes.

Bad Times

Times are getting bad.

Even the angels
pack heat
and have orders
to fire
as the need arises

and the demons
are worse,
killing indiscriminately
without remorse

solitary
or in packs
like wild dogs.

God is Light
so it is said
but even the malls
are dark
and the hungry
city streets
are darker still.

Yet, out in the country,
the little towns
blaze like so
many bonfires
across the vast
continent.

Maybe that is the Light,
the bonfire blaze.

Apocalypse?

What does that
even mean?

The angels and demons
may need to know.

To No Avail

The spider
doesn't care.
Humming birds
make it to South America
when they need to.
Fish go with the flow
until they are eaten
by larger fish.
Only we humans,
using one tenth
of our brain capacity,
try to figure
it all out –
to no avail.

Beat Down By Life

His face was
gnarled as a salt pine
and he walked
with an odd
limp.

His rough hands
told more tales
than he ever did
and that was
quite a few.

He was uglier
than sin
but had a good way
about him,

which must be why
he had so many
women, even
in the later days.

"I've been rode hard
and put away wet,"
he liked to say.

He had a lifetime
of friends
but his best friend
was the bottle.

He went for
the visionary experience.
"I've been beat down
by life but I ain't out yet!"
he would say. "I've got
a sucker punch or two
left in me for sure."

He liked to say
that he could always

see a light at the end
of the tunnel
even if it was a dim light
and a long tunnel.

"Even though you gotta
squint to see it,
don't ever forget
to look for that light,"
he would say.

The last time
I saw him
he was hooked up
to every tube
known to medical
science.
They had taken
both his feet
and one arm
to the elbow.

The nurse said
he wouldn't know
who I was
and she was right.

He was out of
sucker punches
for sure.
But I had to see him
one last time,
even if he didn't
know who I was,

and when I finally
walked out of
the hospital doors
into a suddenly cold
and rainy night,
I was doing a whole lot
of squinting.

The Mick

It was September of 1960.
I was ten going on eleven
and like millions of other boys,
he was my hero,
number seven in pinstripes,
hitting with power
from both sides of the plate.
When he drove
one out of the park,
whether I was seeing
it on TV or hearing it
on the transistor smuggled
into my late night bed,
it took my breath.

The Yanks were in Baltimore
for a three game stand
and I was there for game two
on a fine and golden
late summer Saturday,
my first and only
major league game.
My dad had bought me a real
major league ball for
the Mick to sign.

The Orioles won
2-0 on a Brooks Robinson
home run and took
over first place
but The Mick went 3 for 4.

After the game, my father and I
waited outside the stadium at
the players' gate.
There was only one autograph
I wanted on my ball

and I passed up Kubeck and Berra
and Maris and Ford and all
the others.

The Mick and Hank Bauer
were the last ones out,
each with a woman on his arm.
I was one of the shyest kids
you could ever meet,
but I went right up to The Mick
and asked for his autograph.

The Mick and Bauer
and the two women didn't say a word,
just kept walking across the lot
toward a big black Cadillac and
I walked right beside them.

"Please, Mr. Mantle,
could I have your autograph?"

The Mick never looked at me
and never said a word and neither
did Bauer.

"Please, Mr. Mantle?"

Finally, the woman
holding on to The Mick's arm
blurted out: "I bet you didn't
even root for us!"

"Yes I did!" I cried.
"I might have been
the only one in the whole
stadium, but I did!"
This was a true statement
and I thought it might count for something.

"Please Mr. Mantle..."

The woman didn't
say anything else
and The Mick never even
looked at me
and soon they made it
to the big black Cadillac,
got in and drove away.

"Asshole!" yelled another kid
nearby. "Prick!" screamed
somebody else.

I remember when we got back
to the house where
we were staying in Baltimore,
my Dad and I played
pitch and catch
with my new ball.
The green grass of that yard
reminded me of the green
of the Memorial Stadium outfield
and of The Mick doubling
down the right field line.

It was one of the few times
my Dad ever played with me
like that.

I don't know
what happened
to that major league ball.
I vaguely recall that,
one day, playing
with some friends in the pasture,
I hit a long fly ball
deep into the woods.

If I Could Only Find The Words

I would write you
a little poem.
In that poem,
I would praise you
for the beauty of your
soul, I would tell you
that, late at night,
in the deep quiet,
I can hear the stars
singing your name.

On Thinking About The Impermanence of Things Or Why We Should Make The Most Of Each Day

It wasn't always this way
and it won't always be this way.

This much is for sure.

Just ask Tyrannosaurus Rex
or the Diprotodon.

How long do we have
before the moon
burns up in the sky
and the oceans boil

or dark ash covers the cold land
and the lights go out
for good?

How long do we have
before that little translucent blip
which represents
all our skyscrapers
all our super highways
all our satellites
all our art and philosophy
all our hopes and dreams
blips right off
the cosmic screen?

Winter Moonrise

Silent
as frost,
the pale
and
ancient
orb
slips
slowly
upward,
undeterred
by the
grasping
fingers
of trees.

Simple Things

How odd
that we should
constantly forget
how the simple
things can be
so good
and so much
better than
most anything
else:

the cool drink
of water
from the tap,
the relaxed
conversation
on the porch,
making love
with someone
we love and who loves
us back.

Who, lying
on a death bed,
is going to say:
I wish I had
put in more
hours on the job,
I wish I had made
more money,
I wish I had
spent less time
doing the simple
things?

Whippoorwill

As still as the quiet
flowers of dusk,
the man sits
in the garden
and awaits the cry
of the whippoorwill
from within
the dark woods
of a lost world.

Because the sin
of madness clenches
his heart,
he pretends
to wear a mask,
and it is the mask
of a whippoorwill.

From behind and
from within the mask,
the man questions himself.
The questions spring
from the trembling
of his heart
and from the shadows
in the garden.

The sin of madness is truth
and it speaks
with a fierce voice.
It is the cry
of the whippoorwill
as it shatters the silence
of the woods.
It is the cry of the man
as he shatters
the silence of himself
and the mask
of the whippoorwill

which he has worn
in the confusion
of shadows.

Creative Writing Class Assignment: Write A Poem About Sidewalks In 20 Minutes Or Less

This particular
monster
was bred for
speed and power.
His hunger
was prodigious
and his favorite
delicacy was
sidewalks.

He would devour
them late at night
when there were
fewer of the little
soft, nasty tasting
things to spit out.

3 AM

We live our lives
on the edge
of pain,
occasionally
crossing over
that edge
and needing
band aids
or drugs
or booze
to bring us back.

But we know
real pain,
big pain,
could be just
around the corner
of the next hour,
the next day,
or the next year

when there
might not be
any crossing
back over.

This is why
we sometimes
find ourselves
awake and
wordlessly
holding
each other
so tightly
at 3 AM.

January 2017

From a strange land
of fear and rage

the Beast has come,
wrapped in
a whirlwind of fire.

His tongues of flame
are forked
with glowing brands.

Trumpets sound
and bombs
burst in the air

as the forked tongues
call for the graves
to be opened
and for all the dead
to come forth
in jubilation.

But all the graves
are empty.

Only the eyes of the dead
are left
and they are abroad
in the night

watching in disbelief.

For As Long As You Can

When it's so good
that what you
inexplicably have
becomes
the paradigm,

when it's so good
that you know
the bar is now set
impossibly high,

when it's that good
and you know
the rest will never
measure up…

all you can do
is hold on
with all you've got

and ride that horse,
ride that wave,
ride that magic carpet
for all you're worth

enjoy the wind
in your hair
and smile, smile, smile

for as long
as you can.

About the Author

Kendall Bradley is a native of Accomack County on the Eastern Shore of Virginia. Unlike most Shore natives and many of the "come heres," he does not hunt and fish but nonetheless can appreciate the enduring magic of this narrow spit of land wedged between the Atlantic Ocean and the Chesapeake Bay. Every now and then, he types a few lines on his laptop which sometimes, by a strange alchemy of sorts, are transformed into something that can loosely be termed "poetry." Kendall lives with his lovely wife, muse, and best friend, Ronda, in the small town of Melfa, a community which sprang up when the railroad came through in 1884 and which straddles the now abandoned track and Lankford Highway, a portion of U.S. Route 13 which, it is said, once ran from Maine to Florida and perhaps still does. *Vicinity of Time* is his third book of poetry.

www.ingramcontent.com/pod-product-compliance
Lightning Source LLC
Chambersburg PA
CBHW070856050426
42453CB00012B/2229